Childhood bereavemen

Developing the curriculum

an

Nin

spotLIGHT SERIES

Childhood
Bereavement
Network

national
children's
bureau

Childhood Bereavement Network
The Childhood Bereavement Network brings together organisations and individuals to improve the range and quality of support for bereaved children, young people and their families and care givers.

National Children's Bureau
The National Children's Bureau promotes the interests and well-being of all children and young people across every aspect of their lives. NCB advocates the participation of children and young people in all matters affecting them. NCB challenges disadvantage in childhood.

NCB achieves its mission by:
- ensuring the views of children and young people are listened to and taken into account at all times
- playing an active role in policy development and advocacy
- undertaking high quality research and work from an evidence based perspective
- promoting multidisciplinary, cross-agency partnerships
- identifying, developing and promoting good practice
- disseminating information to professionals, policy makers, parents and children and young people.

NCB has adopted and works within the UN Convention on the Rights of the Child.

Published by the National Children's Bureau, Registered Charity number 258825.
8 Wakley Street, London EC1V 7QE. Tel: 020 7843 6000. Website: www.ncb.org.uk

Reprinted 2005

ISBN 1 904787 14 2

British Library Cataloguing in Publication Data
A catalogue record for this book is available from the British Library

Contents

Foreword

Death is a fact of life. Grief is not an illness; it is a normal and inevitable part of human existence. All children and young people will experience loss and will have to find ways to incorporate its meanings into their lives. Helping children and young people to confront and learn about loss, grief and death and to develop emotional capacity and intelligence is too important to leave until moments of personal or community crisis. The school community has a central role in the task of supporting children, young people and their families. It is the primary focus of social interaction for children and young people and the context in which most of their formal learning occurs. This booklet offers support and advice to schools in the important task of acknowledging and responding to those children and young people facing bereavement, and preparing all children for death through PSHE and Citizenship and other areas of the curriculum.

It can feel very hard to know how best to help children and young people affected by loss. Many adults try to protect children when death occurs. We sometimes hope that by not talking about it we can shield children and young people from sadness and pain. We may feel overwhelmed by our own feelings of grief, or anxious about making things worse for the child or young person by doing or saying 'the wrong thing'. However, attempts to protect children and young people from the truth usually leave them confused and alone with their questions, fears and powerful feelings. We cannot make a world in which children and young people will not experience bereavement. We can offer them support as they do so. Preparing them for bereavement and helping them to express and cope with feelings of sadness, anger, anxiety and loneliness can provide profoundly important lessons that they will take with them for the rest of their lives.

Barbara Monroe
Chair of the Childhood Bereavement Network and
Chief Executive of St Christopher's Hospice

Acknowledgements

Thank you to all the people who were so generous in sharing their knowledge and expertise. This resource is truly a collaborative effort drawing on materials and ideas from, and conversations with, the members of the Childhood Bereavement Network. Thank you to Sarah Parsons and Sharron Williamson who provided the secondary school lesson plans and to Desney Cromey, TreeTops who provided the primary school lesson plans. Thank you also to Sue Plant and Pam Stoat whose original idea was developed into the Changes Timeline lesson plan. We are extremely grateful to the Gatsby Charitable Foundation for funding the development of this booklet.

We also thank the following for their suggestions and case studies:

Jill Adams
Simon Blake
Ann Dent
Jan Goulstone
Anna Khambatta-Perkin
Sarah MacLean
Simon Marsh
Helen Marchant
Barbara Munroe
Hardev Notta
Sue Pentland
Stephanie Quayle
Sacha Richardson
David S Stewart
Di Stubbs
Karen Turner
Maggie Turner

Thank you for Tanya Proctor for editing this booklet so carefully and a special thank you to Tracey Anderson for her excellent administrative support.

Finally we thank all the children and young people and their families who have taught all of us.

1 Introduction

'If you are a teacher, part of it is being very focused on the future, which makes death very worrying.'
Professor Oliver Leaman (1996) quoted by Haigh in TES.

This booklet aims to help teachers and those working in schools to support bereaved children and young people, and to communicate with all children and young people about death and dying. The reasons why schools need to address death, dying and bereavement are clearly set out, and practical ideas are given of how to achieve this through the curriculum as well as pastoral care.

Case studies are included which provide guidance and reinforce what constitutes good practice. Towards the end of the document there are several lesson plans for use in primary and secondary schools, and the booklet ends with a section on useful contacts and resources.

The resource draws on best practice and expertise across the Childhood Bereavement Network (CBN) and colleagues working in and with schools. There are quotes from children and young people throughout the text. Most of these children and young people participated in two videos produced by the Childhood Bereavement Network: *You'll always remember them, even when you're old* offers views and opinions of children aged 6 to 12; and *A death in the lives of...* offers views and opinions of young people aged 13 to 16 (see resources section for details). Some of these children also took part in the participation video which accompanies the Participation Guidance published by the National Healthy Schools Standard.

2 What is bereavement?

Definitions

- Bereavement describes the loss that people experience when someone close to them dies.
- Grief describes the emotions that people go through as a result of the loss of someone close to them.
- Mourning describes the period of time when people are grieving.

Childhood bereavement: some basic facts

The following facts have been supplied by Winston's Wish (a charity providing support for bereaved children and young people):

- Every 30 minutes in the UK, a child under 18 is bereaved of a parent. This equates to 53 children a day and almost 20,000 per year.
- Three per cent of 5 to 15 year olds have experienced the death of a parent or sibling – this equates to about 255,000 young people in the UK.
- Sixty seven per cent of the children supported by Winston's Wish in 2001-2002 had experienced the death of a parent. Sixty two per cent of the children and young people supported had been bereaved by a sudden death.

- Research indicates that if a bereaved child is not supported adequately, they are likely to experience a loss of self-esteem, which may take up to two years to become evident.

How do children and young people express grief?

Children and young people are likely to go through a range of emotions when someone dies. The ways in which they respond to a death are largely determined by their age, their understanding of death, their relationship with the person who has died, the circumstances of the death and the way that the death is dealt with by others around them.

- It is generally agreed that children under the age of two years will experience a sense of loss and seek out the presence of the person who has died, but that intellectually they will be unable to comprehend the permanence of their loss.
- Children aged two to five years may have an awareness that 'death exists,' but they may not understand the permanency of death and think that the person who has died will eventually return.
- Children between five and nine years have a greater understanding of death: they have started to understand that death is permanent and irreversible. They may struggle to understand their emotional response to the death, which can include feelings of guilt and fear.
- Children aged nine to 12 will understand the finality of death, which may make them more aware of their own mortality. They may deny feelings of loss and be trying to 'get on with their life'.
- Adolescents are likely to grieve in similar ways to adults. In some cases they experience very powerful emotions which have a profound effect on them and can result in them questioning their own identity or having suicidal thoughts.

Some of the usual grief reactions that you might witness in a bereaved child in the classroom, or that you might be told about, include:

- difficulty attending school
- anxiety
- sadness and longing
- anger and acting-out behaviour
- problems in school often related to difficulties concentrating
- physical complaints, such as headaches or stomach upsets
- guilt, self-reproach and shame
- vivid memories
- sleep difficulties (Dyregrov 1990).

Children and young people do not grieve all the time and will have times when they have fun – indeed adolescents may express a need to have a 'normal life with their friends' – but in time and with support most children and young people recover from bereavement. However, for a small minority of children who are already vulnerable or experiencing family difficulties, bereavement may be the 'final straw'. For these children, bereavement places them at increased risk of poor mental health, exclusion from school and becoming involved in criminal behaviour.

Research also suggests that children and young people who have been bereaved are more likely to smoke, drink alcohol and use drugs. Children and young people who are bereaved suddenly and violently have been identified as being particularly at risk, with those who witness the manner of death being more disadvantaged (Harrison 2001).

3 Why should schools address bereavement?

'It's important that the teachers listen to children because they might be upset but they can't tell anybody because no-one wants to listen'
Andrew

At any given time up to 70 per cent of schools are dealing with a bereaved child (Holland 1993). Despite this, some schools do not address death and dying, nor have they thought about or developed a response system that enables them to respond to bereavements experienced by children and young people (Holland 2001). Many teachers feel inadequately trained and are anxious about supporting bereaved children and young people in their care (Leckey 1991).

Current educational guidance emphasises the need for schools to promote emotional health and well-being and inclusion, and to address inequalities as a strategy for raising standards. This is based on research evidence that shows that when children and young people feel healthy, happy, supported and loved, they are more likely to be able to reach their full potential at school and in other areas of their lives.

Bereavement can have a stigmatising and excluding effect on the lives of children and young people. They may feel different from their peers and isolated from their school and education as a result. Some bereaved children and young people have found that their peers bully them. In addition their home, emotional and material circumstances may change as a direct consequence of the bereavement. These and other factors mean that a bereaved child may also experience short or long-term difficulties at school.

Children and young people feel that there is widespread reticence about including death and bereavement as topics within the curriculum. They have much greater experience of bereavement and loss than adults tend to perceive, and most feel that death and dying should be addressed by schools from primary level upwards (Jackson and Colwell 2001; and Kenny 1998).

The Childhood Bereavement Network recently undertook a video participation project which captures on film the views and voices of children and young people who have been bereaved. They report that although there are some schools that are very supportive, some teachers and staff at best ignore their bereavement and at worst make inappropriate remarks.

'She wouldn't let me make a Father's Day card. It wasn't fair, I do have a father I just can't see him.'
Andrew

There is a clear guidance framework to support schools covering death and bereavement. The Education Act (1996) stresses the importance of promoting the personal, social and spiritual development of children and young people as part of their education; this would necessarily include discussion of the life and death continuum. The national Personal, Social and Health Education (PSHE) and Citizenship Framework (DfEE and QCA 1999 a and b) also stress the need for schools to address bereavement specifically as well as other losses such as divorce and separation.

Schools and teachers are trusted and familiar organisations, and individuals operate in a familiar daily routine. Therefore schools are well placed to help children and young people explore and develop an awareness and understanding of death as well as supporting bereaved children and young people. Schools also have an invaluable role in supporting a bereaved child's peer group to cope with the death. While many children and young people say that their friends have been supportive, others report that the difference of having experienced death isolates them from their peer group, and that other children and young people's reactions have been hurtful and stigmatising (Cross 2002).

'Everyone was teasing me. They were saying you haven't got a dad and pointing at me.'
Annie

How can schools address bereavement?

Schools can address the issue of bereavement in two ways:

- as part of PSHE and Citizenship, which will involve the inclusion of death and bereavement as topics in the curriculum (Holland 2001)
- as part of pastoral care, which will involve helping a bereaved child or young person through their grieving

Schools that develop a policy clarify how death and bereavement issues are managed pastorally as well as in PSHE and Citizenship.

Adults who offer support in school and deliver lessons on death, dying and bereavement may be teachers, support staff, learning mentors, Connexions personal advisors, health professionals or counsellors.

'My teacher was very nice. Her parents have died so she knew all about it.'
Annie

In addition, all childhood bereavement services across the country offer support to children, young people and their families. Many of them offer advice on how to teach children about death and bereavement, as well as on the type of support they need. Unfortunately, not all areas have a bereavement service. Information about open access services in England, which support children and young people and their families what ever the cause of death, can be found on the CBN website (www.ncb.org.uk/cbn/directory/index.asp).

PSHE and Citizenship

Include bereavement in the PSHE and Citizenship Policy and other whole-school policies for example behaviour and bullying

School policies should detail the school ethos in relation to addressing bereavement and the issues arising from it from a pastoral and curriculum perspective. This will clarify good practice in the event of a death occurring within the school community and guide staff effectively around the many challenges bereavement will pose. It will also support staff to include death and bereavement in planning and delivering PSHE and Citizenship.

Death should be part of the curriculum

Incorporating teaching and learning about loss, change, death and bereavement into the curriculum identifies it as being a natural process of life just as birth, sex and relationships are. Opportunities that arise naturally (such as flowers wilting and dying, or school pets dying) can be used as a catalyst for discussion. This can happen in obvious areas such as PSHE and Citizenship and science, but also in subject areas such as English, history, geography and religious education, which can address different beliefs and cultural traditions regarding death.

Put death and bereavement on the staff training agenda

Local bereavement services are a real resource to a school and can either deliver or advise on training. The Childhood Bereavement Network provides a directory of childhood bereavement services (see resource section for details of organisations that may be able to help www.ncb.org.uk/cbn/directory/index.asp). In addition the Educational Psychology Service, the school nurse, school counsellor, local healthy school co-ordinators or young people's health advisory services or the local PSHE and Citizenship advisor may also be able to support this area of work. Faith and non-faith schools may utilise the skills of local religious or faith personnel. Training in relation to the experience and understanding of death by children and young people will help teachers and schools to relate to bereaved children and young people and to teach others about bereavement issues with confidence.

Pastoral care and support

Winston's Wish, a member of the Childhood Bereavement Network, has endorsed the following responses as constituting good practice in being supportive of bereaved children within school.

Make time to talk to the bereaved child

Explicitly acknowledge the child's loss. Use the name of the person who has died, suggest that talking can sometimes help and say that you are available. Saying nothing gives the message that this major event in their lives is not important and that you can do nothing. As long as you ensure that the child has a choice about listening or talking, you can't do any harm by addressing the issue.

'They think that after a month or so you're ok…and you have to tell them that you're not.'
Luke

Acknowledge feelings and talk about memories

When doing this, remember that not all relationships are happy and loving; a child might be experiencing some sense of relief if they have had a difficult or abusive relationship with the person who has died, so be prepared to talk about the good and not so good with the child. It may be helpful to encourage the child to make a memory box.

Always use the correct terminology

Use terms such as 'death', 'die', 'died'. Avoid using euphemistic terms such as 'gone away', 'lost' or 'sleeping' which might only confuse the child about how the death came about and its permanency. Accurate language helps a child understand that the death is permanent and will prevent them worrying about dying themselves. This applies in both pastoral and curriculum contexts.

Give honest answers

Grieving children and young people deserve and are entitled to honest and straightforward answers. They are often curious about death and burial. Teachers should answer questions factually as far as possible and avoid making value judgments. They should ensure that they are aware of the family's cultural and religious beliefs so as not to confuse the child by providing conflicting information.

Involve bereaved children

It is important to involve the bereaved child in decisions about how the school manages issues relating to their loss. Talk to the child about their preferred way of informing their peers about what has happened and about the support they need and want.

Be aware of any changes in the child's behaviour

Bereaved children and young people often experience a loss of concentration and focus and this may affect their learning at school. They may be aggressive in the classroom or playground, potentially indicating feelings of anger. Others may be withdrawn and hard to engage and some may 'seem to be recovering well' but actually be finding it hard to find a way of expressing their feelings about what has happened.

Two groups within the school community likely to have experienced a multiplicity of loss, trauma and change are refugee children and children in public care. It is also our experience that pupils in special schools seem to experience a higher incidence of death of their fellow pupils and within their families. Schools need to consider carefully how to offer adequate and on-going support in relation to these issues and may need to consult external expert agencies for further information (see useful contacts).

Similar levels of care should be exercised in relation to children and young people who are bereaved as the result of a suicide or other type of violent death. Be aware that they may be fearful and reticent about sharing information about what has happened, and their feelings related to it, for fear of being stigmatised.

Cultural aspects of bereavement

Hardev Notta from Acorns Children's Hospice who supports bereaved children and young people and their families from Sikh, Muslim and Hindu communities provides the following section on cultural aspects of bereavement.

It is important to talk with and listen to the child and their family and ask them what they need and want. All communities have established rituals, which help them to express grief and manage bereavement.

Many Sikh, Hindu and Muslim families want to prepare their relative for burial or cremation by bathing, anointing and dressing the body themselves. Men wash a male relative and women wash a female relative. Children and young people participate in some way in the funeral. The mourning period varies from family to family and may last from three days to 40 weeks.

During this period the bereaved relatives will stay at home and be supported by other family members and friends who visit to offer support, pay respects and to pray together. Some families will want the children to stay at home and others will want them to return to school before this initial period of mourning is over.

Teachers and friends from different cultures may want to go to the funeral. It is best to ask a family member about what dress should be worn, what colours are suitable and what colours should be avoided, whether heads should be covered and shoes taken off and whether men and women are expected to sit separately. Red is never worn at funerals.

Some families will want their children to go back to their family's original country to attend a funeral and participate in mourning rituals. Generally this, of course, is helpful but sometimes it can difficult because they are expected to join in with something that feels very different from their lives in England. One example is a child who was very upset when he attended his uncle's funeral where his body was placed on a pyre, and set alight in the open cremation area.

It is equally important that assemblies, lessons on death and bereavement in PSHE and Citizenship, religious education and other subjects always offer a cultural perspective which is respectful, sensitive and inclusive.

Teachers have found that it is useful to consider the question *what is culture* and to understand that all people have a culture, which informs all aspects of their lives. Once this is understood and accepted it is possible to ensure that the diverse ways of experiencing and responding to death and bereavement are considered as the norm when teaching and learning about death, dying and bereavement.

Schools have found a dedicated room for meditation, reflection or prayers invaluable.

4 Teaching and learning about bereavement

'Teaching you about death makes you into a citizen because then you've got a value for life.'
Roland

The curriculum presents many opportunities through which death and bereavement can be easily explored. Learning about death will help children and young people to be better prepared for the experience of death and the responses associated with it in the event of an actual bereavement occurring. This learning will be valuable in developing the emotional literacy of children and young people directly affected by the death, giving them greater understanding of their feelings, and increasing their ability to seek support. It will also have an impact on the response of their peers, making them more likely to be sympathetic and less likely to stigmatise the bereaved child or young person.

Education about death and bereavement takes place within the context of education for life in a multicultural society. Issues such as disability, ethnicity, gender, faith and HIV will be raised and need to be discussed sensitively and appropriately within the various subject areas outlined below. Consideration needs to be given to the fact that some children and young people may be directly or indirectly affected by these issues and may have direct bereavement experiences or fears (such as being socially stigmatised because of the nature of the death) that relate directly to them. This may impact upon their ability and willingness to participate in education of this nature. Some children and young people will come from families that have strong religious and cultural views about how death is addressed and bereavement is supported. Teachers need to work carefully with families so that they can support their child appropriately.

When exploring the issue of death in the classroom it is important to be aware of any children and young people or colleagues who have experienced a recent bereavement. Be sensitive to their feelings and needs, and talk through the ideas for study with them before the lesson, making changes if necessary. Children and young people will respond in uniquely different ways to bereavement, and they will want those around them to react differently. Some children and young people report that they want to be able to tell their peer group themselves, others will want their teachers to talk to their classmates. Others will only want their immediate peer group to be aware of the death.

It is good practice to involve parents/carers and children and young people in the development of PSHE and Citizenship. It is also important to talk with children and young people and their families about the ways in which care and support will be provided for the bereaved child in school.

PSHE and Citizenship

Bereavement is a whole-school issue, which is taught and learnt as part of PSHE and Citizenship and healthy school development.

The Framework for PSHE (DfEE and QCA 1999 a and b) states that pupils at Key Stage 3 should be taught to recognise the stages of emotions associated with the loss and change caused by death, divorce, separation and new family members, and how to deal positively with the strength of their feelings in different situations.

At Key Stages 1, 2, 3 and 4 the PSHE Framework provides a broad framework to help pupils 'to lead confident, healthy and responsible lives' through three strands:

- developing confidence and responsibility and making the most of their abilities
- developing a healthy and safe lifestyle
- developing good relationships and respecting differences between people.

In Key Stage 1 (four to seven years) and Key Stage 2 (seven to 11 years), a further aim is to help pupils prepare to play an active role as citizens.

At Key Stage 3 (11 to 14 years) and Key Stage 4 (14 to 16 years) statutory citizenship has three further aims:

- knowledge and understanding about becoming informed citizens
- developing skills of enquiry and communication
- developing skills of participation and responsible action.

This broad framework of PSHE and Citizenship is being developed in schools as part of the school improvement agenda.

The National Healthy School Standard is increasingly used as the main delivery vehicle for the development of PSHE and Citizenship. A national, regional and local infrastructure of support helps schools to develop as healthy schools. Each local education authority (LEA) is involved in a local healthy schools partnership with colleagues from Primary Care Trusts (PCTs) and a range of other agencies.

Teachers, school staff, children, young people and wider community partners work together to develop a healthy school ethos, which involves evidencing their work against a set of criteria.

Bereavement fits into three National Healthy School standard themes: provision of pupil support services, emotional health and well being, and safety.

Provision of pupil support services

Children and young people learn about the support that is available to them, within school and in the school's wider community, to help them manage issues relating to bereavement and death. Outside visitors from bereavement organisations can be invited to participate, and give information about help-line numbers and websites, teach in the classroom and offer support to individual children and young people. The school nurse, educational psychology service, Behaviour Education Support Teams (BEST), Child and Adolescent Mental Health Services (CAMHS), Primary Care Team (PCT) and the Childhood Bereavement Network (see resources section) can also provide information about support services available to children and young people in the event of bereavement. All schools should publicise ChildLine, a telephone service which supports all children and young people 0800 11 11, 0800 40 02 22 (deaf/hearing impaired) or 0800 88 44 44 (children and young people in care).

Emotional health and well-being

Feelings associated with change and transition are discussed and strategies developed to help manage bereavement more effectively. It's also helpful to consider other people's experiences of change and loss, such as those related to migration, refugees and asylum-seeking, and disability. Bullying is a key issue for bereaved children and young people and needs to be properly considered. Moral issues relating to death can be explored within the context of developing an understanding that each person's views, attitudes and beliefs will be culturally determined. Some bereaved children and young people experience additional loss because they have to move to another area to live with other relatives or move to a smaller house because of loss of income from the parent who has died.

Safety

Health and safety and risk assessment issues are explored within a context of developing a healthy, safer lifestyle. Children and young people are enabled to explore their own feelings and fears about death and the process of bereavement, and to explore making informed choices in relation to drug use and unsafe sex, as a way of developing an understanding of the possible consequences of decision-making. HIV could be explored in this context.

Opportunities for addressing bereavement in the taught curriculum

Literacy

Reading, listening and talking about stories or poems about death, dying and bereavement are helpful.

English

Death can be explored through discussion; reading and responding to media articles, stories or poems about death; reading and writing epitaphs and letters of sympathy; exploring feelings and language that are associated with death.

History and geography

These subject areas provide obvious opportunities to explore and compare how different cultures in different locations and times deal with death. Issues such as wars, famine and disasters, population size, life expectancy and the death rates in different parts of the world provide other avenues of exploration.

Science

Death falls neatly into the study area that relates to life processes, for example conditions for plant and animal survival. Issues relating to life expectancy and old age such as medical and scientific advances, and the moral and ethical issues potentially raised by these, could be further developed in PSHE and Citizenship and religious education.

Religious education

Children and young people are often very interested in reading about and talking to members of different faith communities to help them understand the beliefs and practices that relate to death from religious and non-religious perspectives. Pupils are encouraged to express their own beliefs about death and to consider how people care for dying people and remember those that have died. Reflective work relating to 'the meaning of life' and a personal sense of mortality can be facilitated. Moral issues such as abortion, euthanasia, genetic engineering, cryonics, cloning, vivisection, drugs, suicide and murder can be examined and debated in further detail.

Opportunities for bereavement support

Circle and tutor time can be used to safely explore ideas or feelings associated with death and bereavement. School assemblies can provide opportunities for pupils to remember and commemorate people who have died, and to collectively reflect on issues relating to death. When appropriate, prayers for the dead and those who are bereaved may be included in assemblies.

The school nurse, counsellor or personal advisor may be able to provide confidential individual and group support to bereaved children and young people, and can provide input to PSHE and Citizenship lessons on the subject. They will also be able to link children and young people and the school community with local primary care teams, local childhood bereavement services, practice nurses and GPs who will have direct experience of supporting bereaved children, young people and families, sometimes over several generations of the same family.

Some secondary schools are working with Primary Care Trust (PCT) colleagues and voluntary agencies to develop health advisory services in school or in the community near to the school. The staff from these services will offer individual and confidential support to children and young people and may well advise on the planning of relevant PSHE and Citizenship and pastoral support in school.

Peer support

Peer group support can be provided in school through peer listening services, peer education and mentoring initiatives in which children and young people are trained to listen to and support their peers through unhappy or difficult times. Peer support has a positive impact on fostering a climate of support and encouragement within the school community.

'If they have got someone to talk to, that person could go to the teacher...and say could give them a bit of leeway.'
Jonathon

A number of children and young people's bereavement organisations have established peer support forums, groups or websites where young people who have been bereaved can come together and discuss their feelings and experiences. See the resources section for details.

In 2004 the DfES will distribute guidance on participation, which will help schools to ensure that children and young people participate fully in the life of their school. This principle is already addressed by the National Healthy School Standard, which requires healthy schools to ensure that children and young people are actively involved in running their school and helping each other.

Approaches for undertaking the work

Drama – role-play real life scenarios in small groups to develop communication skills around the issue.

Art – painting, collage, 'draw and write' and design as mediums through which feelings and, concerns about death and bereavement can be safely expressed and explored.

Music – creating pieces of music for ritualistic purposes or to express feelings associated with life and death.

Creative writing – creation of poems, articles or word pictures to explore and express feelings and emotions associated with death.

Reading – newspaper articles or books with a theme or message related to death and bereavement. Involve children and young people in collecting and developing some core literature concerning death for the school library aimed at pupils, teachers and adults. Quiet opportunities for reading and reflection could be facilitated.

Circle time – provide opportunities to share feelings in a safe environment and develop empathy for others.

Summary

There may be no legal obligation placed upon schools to address issues of death and bereavement, but there are compelling reasons why they should do so. Opportunities for learning about death are provided through Citizenship, now a statutory subject at Key Stage 3 and 4, and PSHE throughout all Key Stages. In addition, there is clear evidence of the impact of bereavement on a child's ability to learn and fully participate in school.

Many schools have strong and established support structures. The DfES and NHSS are supporting schools to develop the emotional health and well-being of children, young people and staff in school through providing guidance and training (see resources section). All schools want to ensure that children and young people feel safe and supported in school to learn and fulfil their potential.

5   Making it real

This section begins with a poem, followed by four case studies, and ends with step-by-step advice on how to support a bereaved child.

These case studies describe how four schools have managed bereavement. Examples from two primary schools are included so as to provide the perspectives of both a faith and a secular school. At the end of each case study, the school involved identifies its significant learning for further consideration. Di Stubbs from Winston's Wish concludes this section and offers advice to schools on how to offer support to a child or young person and to their family when a parent has died.

In his poem, Lemuel Knights, age 9, helps us to understand a child's grief. Children and young people consistently tell us that opportunities to write poems, draw pictures and express their feelings help them to remember the person they love and find the strength to move on in their lives.

I wrote this poem for my dad, who died on 8th January 2003 of a heart attack. He was born in Trinidad in 1950. The poem is about all the things he loved.

My Christmas Wish

Fried chicken and rice 'n' peas,
hot showers that burnt his knees,
Caribbean rum and good red wine,
and hugs from us all the time.
My Christmas wish that I'm making
this year is for dad to have these
and my dad to be here.

Trees and birds and things like that,
Brian Laras left handed bat,
Caribbean Sunsets over the sea,
and Wicked dancing performed me.

My christmas wish that I'm making
this year is for dad to see these
and my dad to be here.

Bob marley's redemption song,
his crackly radio all night long,
the singing of birds that never ends,
to hear his own jokes,
and the laughter of friends.

My christmas wish that I'm making
this year is for dad to see these
and my dad to be near.

By Lemuel J. Knights

Oakdale Junior School

Oakdale Junior School in Redbridge shares its experience of bereavement as a result of the death of its popular and long-term head teacher.

The last memory held by the majority of the school community is of their much-loved head teacher looking well and happy at the end of a successful academic year and Ofsted inspection period. However, by the end of the first week of the summer holidays the head teacher had been hospitalised and was subject thereafter to extensive diagnostic tests and treatments. It became apparent that he would not be returning to school at the start of the autumn term. Although a recovery was hoped for, the head died halfway through the autumn term.

Management of the period of illness and the death by the school

All the stages outlined below were co-ordinated and managed by the appointed acting head teacher, who had been working at Oakdale for 13 years.

At the start of the autumn term parents, carers, children and young people were informed that the head teacher was very unwell through whole-school assemblies, letters being sent home and articles in the school newsletter.

As it became apparent that the head teacher would not recover and would die, the acting head teacher wrote a letter to all members of the school community informing them of the nature of the head teacher's illness and that he was going to die. The letter was sent home to parents and carers and read out to pupils during assembly. The children expressed shock and distress.

The assembly was followed immediately by a brief circle time in class groups when children and young people were encouraged to talk about how they felt, ask any questions they wanted to, and share any thoughts and feelings they had about death and what was happening.

It was made clear that it was fine for anyone to cry and so children and young people were able to see teachers, parents and carers crying in front of other people, thus validating their feelings of sadness.

The head teacher died on a Saturday. Before school on the Monday morning teachers went into the playground to talk to parents and carers as they dropped their children off. As soon as school started, the children were called into assembly and told that the head had died. The acting head teacher relayed the whole story of the head teacher's illness to the school and asked the children to think of a special way in which they could remember him. The children once again went into circle time. All parents and carers were contacted about the death. The school was closed on the day of the funeral. Shortly afterwards the school began attempts to return to usual routines.

Several remembrance activities began immediately:

- A memory tree was created during the week following the head teacher's death. It was made up of paper leaves that pupils, school staff, parents and ex-pupils wrote on expressing their feelings and memories of the head. The tree was completed in a memorial assembly, which was attended by the head teacher's family. Some of the leaves were read aloud and children and staff recounted their memories, which were often amusing, of the head teacher. The tree stayed up in the assembly hall for six months after which the leaves were placed in an album and left in the entrance hall for people to read.

- A memory board was created around the nameplate removed from the head teacher's office. It contained cards, photos and memories that people wanted to share and could be read by anyone. It remained in place for two months.

- Assemblies about grieving were held and all the emotion being experienced was validated through these and on-going circle time work.

- The school community agreed on a commemorative activity, a special 'calm' garden that was developed and named after the head teacher. The garden was decorated with mosaics made by children and young people. It is largely cared for by the children who remain protective of it. Donations and parent teacher association fund-raising funded it. The garden was officially opened through two events: one for adults and one for children and young people, both attended by the head teacher's wife, who was presented with the album of collected leaves.

- A memorial assembly was held at the school on the anniversary of the head teacher's death. This was followed by circle time for the children and young people who knew him.

Although the whole school community was affected by the death, two particular groups of children and young people were identified as vulnerable and highlighted for 'special care' in the period immediately following his death and since then: a group of six pupils who had been bereaved as a result of the death of one of their parents; and those 'challenging' children who had been given extra emotional support by the head.

Learning points

Having steered a school through this process, the acting head teacher identified the following points as warranting consideration by other schools:

- Provide clear and accurate information to all members of the school community about what is happening by using appropriate and unambiguous language.
- Create opportunities for all members of the school community to express their feelings: encourage openness and honesty about feelings.
- Accept any comments children and young people make about death and dying as valid, given their experience and understanding.
- Use books and poems as well as creative and expressive activities to encourage expression of feelings.
- Allow people to have space and time. Accept that the grieving process takes time.

- Ensure that the person managing and co-ordinating this process is adequately supported. This support might come from other members of staff within the school, from LEA advisors or external peer support groups such as a head teachers' group.

Up until the time of the death of the head teacher, the issue of death and bereavement had not been one that had been explicitly addressed through the curriculum. Fortunately the head had created and left a legacy of an open, supportive culture within the school, which had created a strong sense of community and facilitated open expressions of grief and widespread use of circle time. This caring environment has been further developed and death and grief are addressed openly.

St Mary Magdalene School

St Mary Magdalene is a Church of England primary school in Islington, North London. In this case study staff share their experiences of managing two recent bereavements: the first was the death of a pupil from year 6, and the second the death of the long-standing school secretary.

The school is a multi-ethnic inner-city school whose faith perspective permeates all areas and aspects of school life. This perspective took on particular significance to the whole school community during the bereavements, when the faith of the staff and pupils was of particular help to them.

Management of the deaths by the school

The head teacher, who had experience of bereavement counselling, led the process adopted by the school to help them manage this time. He was also able to draw on the considerable resources and experience of the personnel of two churches involved with the school.

After the school had learned about the death of the pupil, and the facts relating to the death, two events took place in parallel. Parents and carers were invited to meet with the head teacher in the school hall, and class teachers met with the children and young people in their class setting. Both groups were told what had happened to the pupil and that he had died. A school assembly followed this for all the children and young people and then a joint parent, carer and child assembly was held the following day. This provided the school community with an opportunity to cry together, acknowledge their loss and remember the child involved.

The school produced a remembrance book, which commemorated the life of the pupil. Children and young people contributed paintings, drawings, poems and pieces of writing that spoke about their feelings about the child and what had happened. The funeral took place during the Christmas holidays. Lots of the teachers and pupils attended.

Two months after the child's death a memorial service was held in the school church. At this point it became evident that many of the children and young people felt very angry about what had happened and that lots of feelings had been bottled up. A trauma counsellor was brought into the school to work with the children in class groups, and individually with children and their families. A bench with a dedicated plaque was installed in the school grounds three months later, accompanied by a brief ceremony, which the bereaved family attended.

St Mary Magdalene School is clear that being a faith school and having a particular perspective on life and death was helpful. The perspective allowed pupils to understand death as something that is ultimately inevitable and part of the cycle of life. Some months after the death of the pupil the school secretary died. She had been ill for a short time before she died, and this gave pupils a realisation that people don't always recover from illness and also showed them the perspective of death as being a release from pain.

The two deaths became linked – 'they'll meet each other in heaven' was a commonly heard comment, and the second death brought back the memories of the first bereavement.

Learning points

The head teacher identified the following points for consideration by other schools in relation to working with issues of death and bereavement. While some points might seem to be of particular pertinence to faith schools, they all relate to and can be applied within secular schools:

- In the event of a death happening, ensure that the school community actually talks about the death – not to do so to some extent denies the value of the person who has died, and also denies children the reality of the situation.
- Be clear, open and honest about what has happened.
- Provide opportunities for and encourage children and young people to express their feelings openly. Make use of poems, drawing and painting to help this. Honour children's feelings by displaying the work they produce if they are happy for that to happen.
- Accept that it is fine for adults to show their grief. Acknowledge and be respectful of the different expressions of grief by people from different cultural and faith backgrounds.
- Draw on the support resources that are available to you as a school. These may come from the wider community, an affiliated church, the local education authority, local bereavement services or local educational psychology services.
- Do not expect things to 'return to normal' too quickly. Accepting a death and grieving takes time.
- Recognise that any significant death in a school community will bring past bereavements to the forefront in the memories of individuals within the school. Schools may therefore have to deal with and be prepared to respond to more than the immediate death.
- Ensure that annual religious festivals are utilised as a way of acknowledging and exploring death, loss and bereavement.
- Ensure that the school has pets. Involve the children and young people in caring for them so that they become aware of the life cycle, including the pet's death (animals such as gerbils and hamsters are relatively short-lived so their death will be a feature in school life).

As a faith school, St Mary Magdalene has sought to cultivate an ethos of openness and honesty in relation to life, death and bereavement. Prior to the deaths of the two members of their school community the school already used opportunities within PSHE and Citizenship and the curriculum to explore issues of death and bereavement with children and young people. This practice continued through the grieving process and continues today.

Shepherd School

Shepherd School is for children and young people (3 to 19) with severe or profound learning disabilities in Nottingham. In this case study the head teacher talks about the significant effect of bereavement on the lives of children and young people with learning disabilities. He also talks about three pupils who experienced bereavement within a three-month period.

Background

Bereavement is a key issue for this particular group of children. Families talk poignantly about the initial bereavement experienced when their child is born. As time moves on there is more acceptance but families still have to deal with other people's comments and attitudes. Children grow up hearing people saying to their families 'oh what a shame'. Both the child and their families have to deal with this continuing expression of loss and bereavement. Children and young people can also experience loss and regret, as they come to realise and understand the extent of their disability.

Some families, carers and school staff believe that disabled children already have too much to deal with and want to protect them from any illness and bereavement in the family or close community. Children with disabilities may have several significant relationships with adults who care for them and are often very distressed when carers or teachers move on to new jobs. Another significant number of the children have degenerative illnesses and watch the increasing illness and even deaths of their friends.

Shepherd School ensures that children and young people and their families are supported through bereavement and prepared for death, dying and bereavement through PSHE and Citizenship and pastoral care. Students are trained as peer supporters and play a crucial role in supporting bereaved friends and students.

'Philip's Dad had died, I was brought in and I was relied on to support him.'
Charlotte

Management of the deaths by the school

The father of a girl aged 11 had been diagnosed with terminal cancer. The mother approached school, as she was very uncertain of the approach to take. Teachers and staff in the school were able to work with the girl who was autistic and her mother to prepare her. Initially the mother was very uncertain as to what her daughter would understand. The school helped her to talk to her daughter. Storybooks were used to help her understand that her father was dying and that it was final. The girl learnt the signs for death and was able to express her distress. There was the opportunity to prepare scrapbooks and memory books of family time together (these would prove invaluable in providing comfort and solace). When her father finally died it was still a shock but she had been prepared for it. There was finality. After his death she became anxious about being away from her mother. There seemed to be a fear that if she came to school, her mother might not be there when she got home. The school worked closely with the mother to alleviate these fears, and to re-integrate her daughter into the life of the school.

The father of a young woman aged 17 died suddenly through suicide. This situation emphasised the importance of including death as part of PSHE and Citizenship because clearly there was no chance to prepare this young woman. She was very upset and experienced powerful mood swings. Staff talked with her and her mother and realised that she needed more specific support.

A counsellor from NSPCC had been working in the school for the previous year or so and had begun to build up her experience in working with children and young people with learning disabilities. Often agencies that might be expected to provide support say that there is no one with experience or expertise in working with disabled children and young people. The relationship, which had been developed with the NSPCC, was to prove invaluable in supporting this young woman. The school organised regular confidential counselling sessions for her with the NSPCC worker.

The father of a boy aged 8 died suddenly of a heart attack. Again, there was no time to prepare him and initially the family wanted to protect him and exclude him from the family's grief and the funeral. The school encouraged and supported the family to involve the boy in the whole process of grief and bereavement including the funeral. This took a great deal of strength by the mother but proved invaluable in the long run because the boy understood that his father had died and would not be coming back. If this boy had not been included in the process, he may have thought that his dad had gone away and left him.

Learning points

Shepherd School has built up a significant knowledge about what to do and how to support children and their families through bereavement. The head teacher stresses that despite their confidence in dealing with bereavement, it is never easy and always painful for everybody. Here he offers some learning points from his considerable experience.

- Be as open and honest as possible with children, young people and their families.
- Ensure that life and death is included as part of the whole life cycle in PSHE and Citizenship.
- Be 'upfront' about disability and help children and their families to express their loss about disability, helping them to express their feelings including anger appropriately.
- Ensure that children and young people who need support with communication are taught signs or symbols, which enable them to express their feelings.

- Include all children and young people in the bereavement process. It is the school's experience that even children and young people with multiple disabilities and limited communication experience loss and somehow know that a particular person is not there.
- Create school events and processes that honour, celebrate and respect each person who is being mourned.
- Include and support parents and keep a special lifeline to those parents who no longer come to the school anymore because their child has died. Shepherd School makes sure that it continues to invite their families to come to the school with an approach, which is supportive. 'We're here, come when you are ready'.
- Give families and staff a leaflet. Shepherd School produces a series of booklets on personal and social issues 'Now they are growing up' one of which is called 'Loss' (see resources section). This leaflet helps parents to think about including children and young people in family bereavement, attending funerals and ways of talking, listening to and helping children and young people through bereavement.
- It's not easy, teachers are human and get upset yet need to stay strong for the children and young people and their families. So don't forget the staff, who will need support when grieving for a child, family member or friend.
- Make sure that staff are well trained and supported. The Laura Centre Family Bereavement Counselling Centre in Leicester has provided training for the Shepherd School staff.
- Schools which experience bereavement often, especially those like Shepherd School, need support as a whole school community. Personal individual letters and support from the LEA and wider school community are very much appreciated.
- Plan a series of processes to help children, young people and staff through the bereavement, which included initial support, a memorial event and remembering individual people with comments such as; 'do you remember when he did…' or 'Look isn't that a lovely photograph of her having a good time last year'. It is important not to forget. Videos and photographs of school events and individuals are invaluable in ensuring that people who have died are remembered.

Cotham School

Cotham is an 11-18, inner city, multi-racial school in Bristol with 1,220 students on role. The school had to find a way of managing and working with the issue of bereavement as a result of the sudden deaths of two members of the school community within a three-month period. The first was the death of a year 9 pupil, and the second a member of staff.

Management of the deaths by the school

The process of helping the school community through the period following both deaths was led by a sub-group from the school's Care and Guidance Management Team. This group includes a range of school professionals who determine the course of action to be taken in the event of a crisis arising. Following the sudden death of the year 9 student, this sub-group led by the vice-principal and including the year 9 team leader, the school's learning mentors and trained student counsellors worked to plan and coordinate the school's response. The group recognised that the whole school was shocked and distressed by the sudden death of one of its students. The process that they went through to help the school community manage this bereavement was as follows.

The group ensured that they obtained accurate facts and information about the death so that the development of rumours and myths around how the death had occurred could be avoided. A list of all the people with whom the information needed to be shared was drawn up and they were duly informed. All school staff knew what had happened. The school governors and the local education authority were informed and involved at all levels.

Arrangements were made for the Care and Guidance Management Team to spend time with all the year groups in the school. During this time, information relating to the death was shared with all students, any questions were answered, and sources of on-going support for the students were identified. Extra time was spent with the year 9 group to which the student had belonged and who were particularly distressed. Although the school site accommodation is limited, space was made available so that distressed students could take time out to read, draw, reflect, write poems and be supported in a safe and secure environment.

The school routinely operates parent interest groups, which are chaired by a parent of a student in the year group and supported by the senior management team. The year 9 parent interest group undertook a lot of work with parents and carers who were both shocked and grieving themselves and anxious to meet the needs of their own children.

The whole school community at Cotham remembered and commemorated the student's birthday, which was shortly after her death, and also the first anniversary of her death. They have on-going contact with the parents of the student who have found the school's remembrance of their daughter to be comforting and significant.

Three months after the death of the year 9 student, a member of the staff team died suddenly. This event was also tragic and shocking but it did not create the same level of widespread distress and 'hysteria' amongst most of the students as the death of their peer had. However, it resulted in massive shock on the part of the other members of staff within the school.

Again the Care and Guidance Management Team went into action. This time it was chaired by the personnel and welfare manager and the clinical psychology team which had the primary aim of offering staff on-going support. The school was officially closed for a day as a way of providing staff with some 'time out' to acknowledge their colleague's death and their grief. It was spent with the family of the member of staff in commemoration and celebration of her life and role and contribution within the school community.

The teacher had a specialist brief for work with students from black and minority ethnic communities. Students she had worked with directly were given additional support. After discussion it was agreed that the students should be told that the teacher had committed suicide. It was in keeping with the school's policy of openness and honesty and acknowledgement of how difficult it often is to cope with death.

Learning points

Having supported the whole school community through these traumatic and difficult events, the vice-principal identified the following points as warranting consideration by other schools:

- Give the whole school community (teaching and support staff, pupils, parents and carers, governors) space and time to acknowledge the death and their grief.
- Recognise that any death has the potential to bring previous experiences of loss, bereavement and pain to the forefront, which can make it difficult for students and staff to find a way of 'managing' the current death. This recognition is critical when supporting teaching staff; teaching requires an element of performance (positive self-portrayal and manner) and this is hard to maintain if painful personal experiences overwhelm them.
- Children and young people affected by death and bereavement grow up and mature rapidly. The experience of Cotham was that the year 9 students matured quickly after the death of their friend and that they effectively became different young people; this has to be acknowledged and worked with.
- Provide on-going access for students, in groups or individually, to school counsellors.
- Rituals and ways of remembering the person who has died are incredibly important and meaningful.
- Ensure that there is adequate support and supervision for the members of staff who lead and manage such a process. It is important that their ability to 'manage' and 'cope' is well resourced in order for them to continue to be sensitive and effective in the process.

At Cotham School, 'coping with loss' was a topic issue taught through PSHE and Citizenship prior to either of the deaths occurring. However, the bereavements experienced by the school highlighted the importance of addressing such an issue in a proactive way. The school has now purchased and makes extensive use of additional resources concerning death and bereavement through the student library. Two resources that have proved particularly effective and popular are *Wise before the Event: coping with crises in schools*, and *A teacher's handbook of death*. See the resources section for full details of both resources.

My dad died but nobody mentioned it

This article written by Di Stubbs of Winston's Wish was published in the first issue of *Spotlight* (November 2003, NCB). It offers advice on how to support a child whose father has died. Winston's Wish believes that bereaved children need education, support and opportunities to express feelings, to communicate with others and to remember.

How can you help?

For most children, simple human caring combined with an awareness of some of the issues that may affect the child's reactions and responses will be enough to make a difference. Some children and young people may need specialist help and support. There are many things you can do to prepare for a death affecting your community and many things you can do in response to a death. First and foremost it is important to be prepared with a clear plan.

The following is a hypothetical situation in a school. The pupil, Jason, is ten years old and he returns to school three days after the unexpected death of his father. It sets out the steps that could helpfully be taken.

When the school is informed of the death

Jason's class teacher (Mr Lee) is informed and arrangements made for someone to cover his class for registration so he can develop a response plan. The rest of the staff is informed. It is agreed how pupils will be told, and previously bereaved children are identified in case they need extra support.

A letter is written for pupils to take home to their parents. Additional information is provided for Jason's classmates which outlines possible reactions and responses from children. This includes helpline support. A letter of condolence is sent to Jason's family.

Before Jason returns to school

Staff are encouraged to acknowledge the death to and with Jason, and to talk with their class about how Jason and his family may be feeling and how they will support him on his return. Pupils explore how they might respond to Jason. Jason's own class and group of friends have a session on feelings connected with death and grief.

Mr Lee visits Jason at home to tell him what has been happening at school and inform him and his family of how the school has been told about his father's death. They agree what will happen on his return to school.

When Jason returns to school

Mr Lee is waiting when Jason arrives and they have some time together. Mr Lee checks that Jason is still happy with the plans for his return to class.

Jason and his teacher identify an adult supporter for him. He is told that he can leave lessons to seek out his chosen supporter when he needs to. Jason and his teacher rejoin the rest of the class and carry out their 'return plan'.

Time is set aside at the end of the day for Jason to spend with Mr Lee, checking out how things have been during the day and to agree a plan for the following morning.

Before the funeral

It is agreed with Jason's family how the school will mark the funeral and any school ceremony. The school ensures that Jason's family knows about any local child bereavement service and also provides information on national services and supports referrals.

Mr Lee compiles a 'calendar of memories' noting any dates where Jason may need extra support – for example, the anniversary of the death, his father's birthday and Father's Day. This calendar can follow Jason through the school and on to his next school. Jason and his family agree with the school over marking Father's Day and other family occasions.

All those who teach Jason identify any areas of heightened sensitivity – for example, if his father died in a fire, studying the Great Fire of London may be difficult.

The head teacher uses a future staff meeting to review events and the school's response, and to plan for any future bereavements.

Summary

Making a commitment to address death and bereavement within the environment of the school is a commonsense, good-practice approach to adopt. Experience and research evidence tell us that children and young people need and are entitled to information and support to enable them to find ways of managing the significant change and disruption in their lives that bereavement and death bring. These very special case studies demonstrate how important it is to have an open and transparent policy. They demonstrate the need to include death and bereavement as part of PSHE and Citizenship to ensure that children and young people are prepared and able to support others as well as get the help that they themselves might need.

It is important to have ongoing support, which needs to last for a long time or at least the time that children and young people need and want the support. All the schools consulted emphasised that it is not a short process and that birthdays and anniversaries of the death should be remembered. Importantly they stress that the staff also need to be able to express their grief and will need ongoing support to enable them to continue to support children, young people and their families through bereavement.

When schools work in partnership with agencies that are able to support their efforts around death and bereavement, they can, as significant institutions in children and young people's lives, make a positive contribution to children and young people's experience of managing these difficult life events.

6 Lesson Plans

This section offers a selection of lesson plans for primary and secondary schools. They are drawn from members of the Childhood Bereavement Network. All the lesson plans can be adapted as a whole or in part and used as ideas for you to develop your own programme.

Please read the booklet before you use these lesson plans to ensure that you are aware of and sensitive to the issues. Be particularly aware of any children or young people who have recently been bereaved in the class before embarking on the lessons. It may be helpful for children and young people who have recently been bereaved to undertake these lessons, but it is essential that they feel safe. Check out your plans for the lessons with them beforehand and make any necessary adjustments.

All teachers will want to ensure that children and young people feel safe by making a working agreement. One group of children agreed to:

- listen to each other
- don't laugh because no question is stupid
- be nice not nasty
- have fun.

Losing something special was developed for use in primary schools by Treetops. The two parts are used sequentially and over two lessons, or could be adapted to be used across several lessons. They are reproduced here with the permission of Treetops.

Changes timeline has been influenced by an idea developed by Sue Plant and Pam Stoate (1989).

What is bereavement? and What kind of support do bereaved young people need? have been adapted from ideas developed by Sarah Parsons (CBN) and Sharon Williams as part of the CBN video resource *A death in the lives of...* Again, these lesson plans can be adapted as a whole or used in part as ideas for you to develop your own programmes.

Losing something special

Lesson aims

- To enable children to understand that everyone experiences a loss at some point in their life.
- To identify and discuss the feelings that accompany loss.
- To develop awareness that all change involves a sense of loss.

Part one

Time

40 minutes

Materials

- Glove puppet
- A copy of the book *Dogger* by Shirley Hughes
- Coloured paper, crayons and pencils

Method

1. Introduce the topic using circle time.

2. Give the glove puppet a name and tell a story about how he lost something special to him. Pass the puppet around the group and ask the children to share experiences of losing something that was special to them.

3. Do another round with the puppet; this time ask the children to say how they think the puppet feels having lost something.

4. Read *Dogger* to the class. Follow the story with a brief discussion about the feelings of the characters in the story.

5. Give out paper, crayons and pencils. Ask the children to draw and, if possible, write a short story about something that they said that they had lost during circle time.

6. Ask them to give their story a title and to write their name on the back of the story. Can they think of anyone else who they would like to read their story? Write down their ideas and staple them to the story.

7. End with a round of circle time, using the puppet to check how the children are feeling after the lesson and before moving on to the next lesson or ending the day.

8. Ensure that they all know how to get further support if they need it: name a teacher or classroom assistant who is able to offer one-to-one support. It may be easier to ask them who the glove puppet could talk to when s/he feels sad in school.

Part two

Time

40 minutes

Materials

- Bambi and Lion King videos (ensure that you have familiarised yourself with the relevant scenes and have the video set at the significant points before the lesson begins).
- Glove puppet or finger puppet (lion, if possible).
- Coloured paper, crayons and pencils.

Method

1. Briefly check what the class recall of lesson one.

2. Inform the children that you are continuing with the same theme and that, as they are probably aware, as well as losing things that are special to us, we also lose a special pet or person when they die.

3. Make a list on the board of all the different deaths the children have experienced, maybe contributing from your own experience or that of other people you know for example pets, relatives, and friends.

4. Show a clip from Bambi that depicts a happy time in his life such as the scene where he skates on the frozen pond. Explain that we have many happy times in our families but that we might also have sad times.

5. Show the scene from the Lion King film that depicts the death of Simba's dad.

6. Pass the glove puppet around the circle and ask the children how they would describe Simba's feelings.

7. Give out paper, crayons and pencils and ask the children to draw a picture of a happy memory that they have of a special pet or person that has died. If they haven't had this experience they can make up their own story and make it into a picture.

8. Ask them to describe what they miss most about that person or pet and why they were so special to them, and help them to write it down on a separate piece of paper.

9. Attach the picture to the words with ribbon and write the child's name on the work. Ask the child to say who they want to read the story and get them to write this on the back of the story.

10. End with a round of circle time, using the puppet to check how the children are feeling after the lesson and what they have learnt, and before moving on to the next lesson or ending the day.

11. Ensure that they all know how to get further support if they need it: name a teacher or classroom assistant who is able to offer one-to-one support. It may be easier to ask them who the glove puppet could talk to when s/he feels sad in school.

Changes timeline

Lesson aim

- To provide children with an opportunity to look at the range of changes that people experience in their lives and to identify the feelings that might be associated with change.

Time

45 minutes

Materials

- Felt-tip pens
- Crayons
- Large sheets of plain paper

Method

1. Ask the children to work in small groups and say what they think of when they hear the word 'change' and record all contributions on a large piece of paper.

2. Ask the group to identify which responses have positive and which negative associations by putting a + or − sign alongside each response? Do some responses have both + and − associations? What does this tell the class about change?

3. Give each child a large sheet of paper and some pens.

4. Ask the children to draw a line on their sheet of paper that can represent their life so far – from birth until now (the line doesn't have to be straight; it can be wavy or jagged – show them some pre-prepared examples).

5. Ask the children to identify the changes that they have already experienced in their lives by marking them on the line. They can draw or write the changes as they like and are able (these might include a new baby in the family, separation of parents, moving house, going to school, milk teeth falling out, death of a pet, losing a favourite toy or the death of someone close to them).

6. Ask the children to find a way of showing which changes felt positive and which negative?

7. Ask the children to get into small groups of three or four and take it in turns to share as much of their timeline as they want to with the other children in their group. Ask the children to talk in their groups and try and answer some of the following questions:

    ✓ Which changes were the most important in their lives and why?
    ✓ What feelings did they experience in relation to the changes?
    ✓ How did they manage these changes?
    ✓ How do they think that the negative experiences could have been made easier to cope with?

8. Ask the small groups to come back together and, after thinking about change in the lesson today, discuss what the word means to them now.

9. Ensure that all children know how to get support if they need it; name a teacher or classroom assistant who is able to offer one-to-one support.

What is bereavement?

Lesson aim

■ To raise awareness and deepen understanding of the effect of bereavement.

Objectives

Students will:
■ discuss and define the terms of bereavement, grief and mourning
■ examine how death is portrayed in the media/popular culture
■ in small groups, discuss the emotions surrounding death and dying and present back to the large group
■ begin work on a poster, based on what has been learnt, to explore some of the feelings/situations raised. This piece of work will be added to in subsequent lessons and will be a visual piece of work linking the lessons and demonstrating learning.

Time

50–60 minutes

Materials

■ Newspaper and magazine clippings covering issues related to death and bereavement. 'Essential Articles' from www.carelpress.com is an excellent resource containing articles on a range of topics, including September 11th, and could be used for this activity.
■ Paper.
■ Pens, pencils, felt tips.

Method

1. Introduce the activity by explaining that the aims of this lesson are to help them explore and develop a better understanding of death and bereavement. Remind the class of the working agreement.

2. Write on the board the words 'grief', 'mourning' and 'bereavement' and ask the young people to think of possible meanings, and differences between the words. This could also be done in small groups or pairs.

3. Encourage students to think about the common uses of terms such as the following 'Stop giving me grief!'; 'You're killing me!'; 'I almost died when he said that…!'

4. What do we mean by these phrases? How are these different from literal meanings? Why are we comfortable with these words in their common, colloquial sense, but not in their true meanings? Do the students feel comfortable talking about the true meanings? Why or why not?

5. Finish off by seeking out dictionary definitions of grief, mourning and bereavement. Discuss how accurate the definitions are in the light of pupil perceptions/previous discussion. Definitions are also on page 3 of this booklet.

Extension activity

1. Split the young people into small groups and give each group a newspaper or magazine clipping. Choose the articles carefully depending on which angle you want to take with the discussion. It might be useful for some students to think about 'natural' death through old age, while others consider sudden and traumatic death through murder or a road crash. It might also be valuable to contrast the death of a child, a sudden death, and death through terminal illness.

2. In their small groups, ask young people to think about the following questions: Who has died? What has happened? Who has been affected? What are the emotions involved? How have people behaved and responded to the death? Is there anything missing that we would like to know? Alternatively, simple questions can be put on the board or written up as a worksheet.

3. Ask the young people to feed their thoughts back to the whole group. Record the young people's thoughts and feedback in relation to the points that you have asked them to discuss on the board. This will serve to validate their responses and clearly identify common themes or experiences that can be explored further through discussion.

4. Invite whole-group discussion of some of the points raised, drawing on both the similarities and differences between different types of death and bereavement, and the feelings involved. Be aware that, particularly where newspaper articles describe the death of well-known people, young people may be distracted from the subject of bereavement.

Closing activity

Ask the young people to think about some of the key words from this session and begin to prepare a poster on a large piece of paper. For example, the sheet could be split into sections to identify how people are affected by death (emotional/behavioural responses); or how to support someone, particularly a young person/friend (listening, sensitivity, thoughtful)? Encourage the young people to express themselves through drawing as well as writing. Explain to them that they will be able to add to their poster as they learn more about bereavement in subsequent lessons.

This activity will give young people a few minutes of quiet, reflective time at the end of what will have been an intense lesson.

What kind of support do bereaved young people need?

Lesson aim

- To deepen understanding of the support needs of young people who have been bereaved.

Objectives

Young people will:
- discuss the personal experiences and views of the young people on the video
- examine the extent to which those views coincide with/differ from their own expectations
- consider the issue of including the topic of 'death' in the curriculum.
- identify what kind of support bereaved young people need.

Time

50–60 minutes

Materials

- TV and video
- A copy of the video 'A Death in the Lives of...' (see resources section for availability)
- Paper
- Pens and pencils

Method

1. Get the group to 'check in' in relation to how they felt after the previous lesson. Revisit the agreements that were made. Adapt the agreement if the group as a whole thinks changes need to be made.

2. Briefly recap definitions of terms from the previous lesson and summarise key aspects covered so far, for example, how we use words about death and dying in everyday life, what they actually mean and how the media portrays death. You might also wish to revisit differences between natural or expected death and sudden and traumatic death.

3. Explain that today's session moves on to consider the views of bereaved young people directly and the kinds of things they felt helped or didn't help them during their bereavement.

4. Watch the relevant section of *A Death in the Lives of...*

   The video is just under 19 minutes long in total, but is divided into sections to facilitate discussion of different issues:

   - support and information from family (7 minutes)
   - what helped (friends, faith, young people's groups) (3 minutes)
   - what didn't help (not enough information, poorly informed teachers) (3 minutes)
   - what can schools do (letting teachers know what has happened; acknowledging the death; including bereavement in the curriculum) (3 minutes 10 seconds)
   - what the young people have learned from their experiences for example, emotional strength and a 'wider outlook' on life (1 minute 35 seconds)
   - the main messages that the young people really wanted to get across to the audience (1 minute).

   The video can be viewed straight through, or could be viewed in sections to break up the session. This is for you to decide, based on the age, ability, nature, and size of the group.

The section headings from the video could be written on the board, or made into a worksheet for young people to take notes during the video. Teachers may like to ask them specific questions such as 'what did the young people in the video think schools should do to help?'; 'What things did the young people say didn't help them?'

General discussion points

5. After watching the video have a discussion about the specific questions the young people were given before watching the video so they can focus their thoughts. The discussion is likely to broaden out into some of the other issues raised in the video, of which there are many. Some questions teachers may like to ask are:

- What did you think about the video?
- Was there anything that surprised you about the video?
- How comfortable did you feel watching the video?
- Which bits were especially interesting for you?

You may also like to discuss the points raised in the video concerning teaching about death in schools, and the extent to which students agree or disagree with the following statements:

'It's kind of ironic because it's the only thing guaranteed in life, but they won't teach you about it.'
Hibba

'Teaching you about death makes you into a citizen because then you've got a value for life.'
Roland

Some young people may openly discuss their personal experiences at this point. However, teachers should be careful to guide the discussion in the direction of support, and could ask the students some relevant questions, such as:

- How supported did you feel?
- Who supported you?
- Could anyone have done anything to support or help you more?

6. Once they have had the opportunity to talk freely about the issues covered in the video, ask them to focus on specific strategies to help someone who has been bereaved. These could include:

- asking if someone is OK
- providing a note in a daily planner for them to leave lessons
- giving extra time to complete homework
- giving the person the opportunity to talk
- not being afraid to show own feelings
- acknowledging the death
- doing 'normal' things
- helping person to have fun
- doing some practical tasks (shopping, cleaning).

Ask them to consider how they would offer support to a bereaved friend or relative. You may want to offer them a role play exercise where one person helps a bereaved young person who is finding it difficult in school. Ensure that everybody 'de-roles' and that learning points from this exercise are identified.

Ensure that all students know how to get further support if they need it. It is useful for young people to identify who can help (friends, classmates, year-group, teachers, head teacher, Connexions personal advisor, school nurse, parents). Young people can add extra information to their existing poster to include ways to help.

Where is support available and what does it look like?

Lesson aim

■ To raise awareness of where they or their friends can access support in the event of bereavement.

Objectives

Young people will:

■ in small groups, research and collate information about the sources of support available for bereaved young people
■ compare results with other members of the class to see the range of services available
■ consider and plan how they would access support and develop more support in school

Time

50–60 minutes

Materials

■ Computers with Internet access or printouts from websites. For example:

www.winstonswish.org.uk
www.childline.org.uk
www.ncb.org.uk/cbn
www.crusebereavementcare.org.uk

www.rd4u.org.uk
www.childbereavement.org.uk
www.jigsaw4u.org.uk

■ Leaflets describing services available locally and nationally, a copy of Yellow Pages, library information leaflets and information on bereavement developed or provided by the local Education Psychology Service.

Optional homework in preparation for this lesson

Young people could talk to parents or other relatives or friends who have been bereaved and ask about the kind of support they received or would have liked to receive.

Method

1. Check in with the class and re-visit the working agreements and how they felt after the last lesson.

2. Recap on the issues discussed in the previous lesson that focused on the kind of support young people need during their bereavement.

3. Introduce the purpose of this lesson, which is to find out what kind of support is available to bereaved children and young people and what form that support takes.

4. If Internet access is available, young people can search for sources of support using search engines. If Internet access is not available, they should be provided with printouts from websites, information leaflets, or adverts from telephone books. Provide a worksheet, or the following questions should be written on the board.

   ■ What information is provided?
   ■ What services are available?
   ■ How can a young person access this information or support?

- What is missing?
- What do you think should be available to young people that isn't at the moment?
- Where do you think services should be provided?
- Who should provide the services?

Ask young people to provide written answers. It is useful to think about these questions in the context of the school, locally in the wider community and nationally.

Ask students to work in small groups to make a plan on how they would both give and get support and what sort of action they will take in school to ensure that bereaved young people get support.

You may like to invite someone in from the local childhood bereavement service, or from the school (personal advisor, learning mentor, school nurse, school counsellor) to talk about the support they can offer.

5. Ask them to add information about support to their existing poster. If they would prefer, they can create a new poster about where it is possible to get help and some general points about what kind of help might be needed.

Extension activity

Having compiled some information from websites, leaflets and local services, and considered their own feelings about death and bereavement, young people can create a bulletin board, display or web page for the rest of the school to see. They may also want to present their work at an assembly or PSHE and Citizenship event to raise awareness among other students at the school.

7 Help, information and resources

Sources of help and information

There are bereavement services for children and young people in most areas of the country. They often provide a range of support to the child and family and will help a school in coping with bereavement and with planning PSHE and Citizenship. The Childhood Bereavement Network (CBN) can provide contact details for these services.

Childhood Bereavement Network
National Children's Bureau
8 Wakley Street
London EC1V 7QE
Telephone: 020 7843 9309
Email: cbn@ncb.org.uk
Website: www.ncb.org.uk/cbn

Childhood Bereavement Network Directory of Open Access Services
Details of childhood bereavement services in England which provide an 'open access' service, working with children and young people whatever the cause of death, can be found at the CBN's Directory of Open Services at www.ncb.org.uk/cbn/directory

Useful contacts

In your local area there are several key contacts who will know what services are available, and will be able to put you in contact with schools that are also addressing bereavement.

National Healthy School Standard

For information on local healthy school partnerships
Telephone: 020 7430 0850
Website: www.wiredforhealth.gov.uk

PSHE and Citizenship Advisor

Contact your local education authority

Health Promotion or Public Health Specialist for children and young people

Contact your local Primary Care Trust

Connexions Partnerships

Telephone: 080 800 13219
Text: 077644 13219
Website: www.connexions.gov.uk

Useful resources

Materials for use in PSHE and Citizenship lessons

Website: *www.teachernet.gov.uk/pshe*
Website: *www.wiredforhealth.gov.uk*

Books for children and young people

A Taste of Blackberries, Buchanan Smith, D (1973) Harper Collins.
A sympathetic account of a friend's death caused by an allergy.

Badger's Parting Gifts, Varley, S (1985) Picture Lions. Story about animals coming to terms with the death of their friend badger and remembering all he has done for them.

Beginnings and Endings with Lifetimes in Between, Mellonie, B and Ingpen, P (1983) Dragonsworld Ltd. A beautifully illustrated book that explains life and death to children.

Come Back Grandma, Limb, S (1995) Red Fox. Explores the close relationship between a little girl and her grandmother who dies.

Dogger, Hughes, S (1993) Red Fox. A story of a little boy who loses his favourite toy.

I can ... You can (2004) A set of four postcards for bereaved children and young people to use as prompts for support from important people in their lives, including teachers and friends. Available from the Childhood Bereavement Network.

Grandpa, Burningham, J (1984) Jonathon Cape. A short story about a young girl's relationship with her grandfather.

Muddles, puddles and sunshine: Your activity book to help when someone has died, Crossley, D (2001) Hawthorn Press. A book full of activities and exercises that offer practical and sensitive support for bereaved children.

Someone close to you has died, (2001) St Christopher's Hospice Publications. For secondary school students. Available from St Christopher's Hospice St Christopher's Hospice, 51-59 Lawrie Park Road, Sydenham, London SE26 6DZ 020 8768 4500 *www.st-christophers.org.uk*

Someone has died suddenly, (1999) St Christopher's Hospice Publications. For secondary school students. Available from St Christopher's Hospice (contact details above)

Someone special has died, (1999) St Christopher's Hospice Publications. For children up to the age of 11. Available from St Christopher's Hospice (contact details above)

Vicki Angel, Wilson, J (2001) Corgi Yearling Books. A poignant story of bereavement and mourning.

Resources for schools

A death in the lives of… (2002) Childhood Bereavement Network. A video resource, which focuses on a group of young people discussing the support that they needed to help them cope with bereavement. Available from: Childhood Bereavement Network Tel: 020 7843 6309

You'll Always Remember them…even when you're old (2003) Childhood Bereavement Network. A video resource, which focuses on a group of children aged 6-12 discussing the support, they received to help them cope with bereavement. Available from Childhood Bereavement Network (contact details above)

Surviving and Thriving (2004) (forthcoming) Childhood Bereavement Network. A video resource in which a group of young people from a range of backgrounds discuss their experiences, achievements and the impact of bereavement on their lives. Available from the Childhood Bereavement Network (contact details above)

A teacher's handbook of death, Jackson, M and Colwell J (2001). Jessica Kingsley Publishers. Available from 116 Pentonville Road, London N1 9JB Tel: 020 7833 2307

Current Issues in PSE: skills for the primary school child, part 2 (2001) Tacade. Available from Old Exchange Building, St Ann's Passage, Manchester M2 6AF Tel: 0161 836 6850

Dealing with Feeling, Rae, T (1998) Lucky Duck Publications. 34 Wellington Park, Bristol BS8 2UW Tel: 0117 9732881 or *www.luckyduck.co.uk*

Finding a way through when someone close has died: What it feels like and what you can do to help yourself: A workbook by young people for young people, Mood, P and Whittaker, L (2001) Jessica Kingsley (Contact details above)

Good Grief 1 teacher's pack – exploring feelings: loss and death with under11's, Ward, B (1993) Teaching pack for use with primary school age pupils. Available from Cruse Bereavement Care, Cruse House, 126 Sheen Road, Richmond, Surrey TW9 1UR Tel: 0870 167 1677

Good Grief 2 teacher's pack – talking and learning about loss and death, Ward, B. Teaching pack for use in secondary schools - Available from Cruse Bereavement Care (Contact details above)

Grief in Children: A handbook for adults, Dyregrov, A (1991) Jessica Kingsley Publishers. (Contact details above)

Ideas for a School Assembly Briefing Paper (2000). Available from: Winston's Wish, Clara Burgess Centre, Bayshill Road, Cheltenham GL50 3AW Tel: 0124 251 5157

Living and Growing Unit 2 (1998) from the Lifecycles series by Channel 4 resources. Available from Channel 4 Learning Tel: 0870 124 6444

Loss (1995) One of a series of *Now they are growing up* for families of children with learning disabilities. Available from Shepherd School, Harvey Road, Bilborough, Nottingham NG8 3BB Tel: 0115 915 3265

Positive responses to death – A strategy for schools information folder. Available from: Winston's Wish (Contact details above)

Seasons for Growth (a loss and grief education training programme for 6- to 18-year-olds).
Contact Notre Dame Centre for Children, Young People and Families, 20 Athole Gardens, Glasgow G12 9BA Tel: 0141 339 2366.

The Social Symbolism of Grief and Mourning, Grainger, R (1998) Jessica Kingsley Publications (Contact details above)

Then, now and always, Stokes, JA (2003) Winston's Wish, The Clara Burgess Centre, Bayshill Road, Cheltenham GL50 3AW Tel: 01242 515 157 www.winstonswish.org.uk

When someone dies: How schools can help bereaved students, Steffes, D (1997), Cruse Bereavement Care (Contact details above)

Wise before the Event: coping with crises in schools, Yule, W and Gold, A (1993) Calouste Gulbenkian Foundation, Central Books, 99 Wallis Road, London E9 5LN Tel: 0845 458 9911

Information and training resources for teachers

Bibliotherapy for Bereaved Children: Healing Reading Jones, E H (2001) Jessica Kingsley Publications (Contact details above). A guide to using texts and reading materials therapeutically with children.

Children and Funerals (2003) A useful leaflet that helps parents think about whether children should have a chance to go to the funeral and how to answer some of their questions. St Christopher's Hospice Candle Project (Contact details above)

Children's Experience of Separation and Loss: information for teachers, Durkin, C and others (2001). Available from Tower Hamlets Educational Psychology Service Tel: 020 7364 4323.

Grief in School Communities – effective support strategies, Rawlings, L (2003) Open University Press, *www.mcgraw-hill.co.uk* A teacher-focused resource that has been well researched, this publication comes highly recommended by St Christopher's Hospice.

Grief in the Family – A video that looks at the ways children and young people respond to grief and what the adults around them can do to help. Could be a useful teacher training aid – Available from Leeds Animation Workshop, 45 Bayswater Road, Leeds LS8 5LF or *www.leedsanimation.demon.co.uk*

Meeting the Needs of Ethnic Minority Children, Including Refugee, Black and Mixed Parentage Children: a handbook for professionals Dwivedi, K (2002) ed Jessica Kingsley Publications (contact details above) Details practical approaches to working with refugee children.

Supporting Refugee Children in 21st Century Britain: a compendium of essential information Rutter, J (2003) Trentham Books. Tel: 01782 745 567 or *www.trentham-books.co.uk* Contains useful information about working with refugee children around loss and trauma.

Supporting bereaved students in primary and secondary school: Practical advice for school staff (2003) Kings College

The Social Curriculum Death and Bereavement Guidance for Schools. Tackling the last taboo: managing bereavement and death in Essex schools (1998). Available from Essex County Council Learning Services, Library and Publications, PO Box 37, Chelmsford CM2 6WN.

References

Cross, S (2002) *I can't stop feeling sad*, *Calls to Childline about bereavement*. ChildLine

Department for Education and Employment and QCA (1999 a) *The National Curriculum: handbook for primary teachers in England: key stages 1 and 2*. DfEE and QCA

Department for Education and Employment (1999b) *The National Curriculum: handbook for Secondary teachers in England: key stages 3 and 4*. DfEE and QCA

Dyregrov, A (1990) *Grief in Children: A Handbook for Adults*. Jessica Kingsley Publishers

Department for Education and Employment (1996) *Education Act.* DfEE

Harrison, R (2001) *Ordinary Days and Shattered Lives: sudden death and the impact on children and families.* Child Bereavement Trust

Holland, J (1993) Child bereavement in Humberside primary schools, *Educational Research* 35, 3, 289-297

Holland, J (2001) *Understanding Children's Experiences of Parental Bereavement.* Jessica Kingsley Publishers

Leckey, (1991) Attitudes and Responses to Death Education of a Sample of Primary School Teachers in Belfast. *Bereavement Care* 10, 22-23

Jackson, M and Colwell, J (2001) Talking to children about death, *Mortality* 6, 3, 321-325

Kenny, C (1998) *A Thanatology of the Child: Children and Young People's Perceptions, Experiences and Understandings of Life, Death and Bereavement*, Quay Books, Mark Allen Publishing Ltd, Jesses Barn, Snow Hill, Dinton, Salisbury SP3 5HN Tel: 01722 716 996

Plant, S and Stoate, P (1989) *Loss and Change: Resources for Use in a Personal and Social Education Programme.* Pergamon Educational Productions

Childhood Bereavement Network Consultant Panel Members

Marie Curie Cancer Care	www.mariecurie.org.uk
Treetops	www.bereavedchild.org
Jigsaw4U	www.jigsaw4u.org.uk
Peace Hospice	www.peacehospice.org
Norwich Primary Care Trust	www.heron.nhs.uk
Barnardo's Orchard Project	Email: orchard.project@ barnardos.org.uk
St Nicholas Hospice	www.st-nicholas-hospice.org.uk
Release, Nightingale House Hospice	www.nightingale-appeal.co.uk
ChildLine	www.childline.org.uk
St Christopher's Hospice	www.stchristophers.org.uk
Acorns Children's Hospice	www.acorns.org.uk
SeeSaw	www.see-saw.org.uk
The Laura Centre	www.thelauracentre.org
Winston's Wish	www.winstonswish.org.uk
The Child Bereavement Trust	www.childbereavement.org.uk
Cruse Bereavement Care	www.crusebereavementcare.org.uk
The Notre Dame Centre, Seasons for Growth	www.notredamecentre.org.uk
Association of Hospice and Specialist Palliative Care Social Workers	www.helpthehospices.org.uk